WITH THIS RING

A Practical Guide for Newlyweds

Renee Bartkowski

Liguori

ONE LIGUORI DRIVE
LIGUORI MO 63057-9999

ISBN 0-89243-430-9
Library of Congress Catalog Card Number: 91:77984

Copyright © 1992, Liguori Publications
Printed in the United States of America
00 01 02 03 04   10 9 8 7 6

To order, call 1-800-325-9521
www.liguori.org
www.catholicbooksonline.com

Cover design by Pam Hummelsheim
Cover photograph by H. Armstrong Roberts

TABLE OF CONTENTS

INTRODUCTION

Most of us grew up with stories that promoted the happy-ever-after myth. "They got married and lived happily ever after." As adults, we know this is a fantasy. But when we're in love, many of us harbor starry-eyed delusions that make us enter marriage with unrealistic expectations.

No matter how well you know each other before marriage, getting married is an eye-opening experience. The knight in shining armor and the princess on the pedestal gradually become two ordinary people with human and ordinary faults and frailties.

Although marriage is an enriching, satisfying, and loving way of life, it is a partnership of two imperfect persons choosing to face life together in an imperfect world. Marriage is a way of life in which everyone stumbles — even outright falls flat. But if you're willing to pick yourselves up and try again — and again — marriage can bring tremendous happiness and fulfillment.

Your marriage is like a house; it must constantly be tended and kept in good condition. Just as a house must be cleaned, repaired, and renovated, so must your marriage be properly and continually maintained. It must be regularly cleaned to remove the residue of selfishness and thoughtlessness, carefully repaired and maintained with patience, understanding, trust, and forgiveness, and painted and repainted with generous doses of love.

A lot of hard work? Yes! But well worth it. If you're willing to invest the needed time and effort, you will build a marriage that is filled with security, companionship, love, and fulfillment. You'll own a true home that is a joy in which to live.

DEVELOPING A SOLID RELATIONSHIP

Don and Sara had been married nearly two years when Sara decided to move out. She could no longer put up with the constant bickering. Outwardly, their relationship appeared harmonious. Seldom, however, could Don and Sara peacefully resolve their differences. Arguments became more intense as the months passed.

Sara cared deeply for Don but decided that the effort, time, and energy it took to remain in the relationship weren't worth the poor results. Their marriage seemed to deteriorate regardless of how hard she worked. Generally, Don did not share Sara's attitude. Regardless of how difficult things were, regardless of how bitter the arguments became, he felt there was always hope.

One evening after a particularly harsh argument, Sara packed her bags and moved back into her parents' home. "There is just no way it's going to work," Sara thought.

Three weeks later, Sara learned that she was pregnant. She reevaluated her marriage and met with Don to discuss giving their relationship another try. The prospect of becoming parents and the emptiness they both felt during the separation renewed their determination to save the marriage.

Their arguing continued during the next few months, but gradually, changes occurred. The couple's determination to make their marriage work motivated them to be more patient and forgiving. By the time their baby was born, Sara and Don had become more willing to cooperate in resolving their differences. They had developed a more solid relationship — an essential to healthy parenting.

Commitment

Nothing much had changed in Don's and Sara's personalities. They had the same faults they'd had from the start, and they still became annoyed with each other. However, a change in their attitudes toward commitment made an overwhelming difference. They became willing to work harder at solving their problems and to give a sufficient amount of time to the problem-solving and healing processes. They learned the essence of the word *commitment.*

Too often, married couples don't give themselves enough time to develop a method of working out their differences within a relationship based on commitment. They become impatient when they run into problems. Instead of accepting the more difficult choice of working toward a resolution, they take the easy way out and give in to defeat. They completely disregard the meaning of commitment.

In the past, social and economic circumstances pressured married persons to make lifelong commitments. With today's changing lifestyles and lighter attitude toward divorce, however, couples often fail to take commitment seriously. Starry-eyed brides and grooms look forward to a life of fun and romance. They fail to realize that marriage, like any lifestyle, brings good days and bad, problems and pleasures, drudgery and delight. In this atmosphere, they must embrace commitment to build a relationship that is fulfilling, enjoyable, mature, responsible, and selfless.

Selflessness

Both Don and Sara found it difficult to achieve and maintain the selflessness demanded of two partners in a marriage. Sara was an only child, the center of her parents' attention. She was accustomed to having her own way. Don had been a popular sports personality in high school and college. He was used to being in the spotlight and receiving the adulation of his fans.

Both had trouble adjusting to married life. No longer was either one of them the center of the universe. No longer did life revolve around their own needs and desires. They had chosen to become two equally important persons in a union that would not possibly survive the stranglehold of self-centeredness.

It took Sara and Don a long time to accept the self-giving dimension of marriage. They had to learn to set aside their own wishes and feelings to tend to the wishes of the other. Their own fatigue, moodiness, and neediness had to take place alongside the fatigue, moodiness, and neediness of their beloved. Living together as wife and husband meant putting their relationship first instead of themselves.

Although Don and Sara didn't always succeed at being self-giving, they accepted their occasional failures without assuming that their marriage was falling apart. A relationship doesn't fail simply because two people run into failures. While both partners are willing to keep on trying, a strong, solid, successful relationship is possible. "We are the ones who are going to make this relationship work" is the attitude that buoys a marriage through turbulent waters.

Respect

Love and determination are not enough, however; respect is another vital ingredient. An intimate relationship not rooted in genuine respect — a respect that accepts the shortcomings and gifts of self and other — has nothing to fall back on when love wearies.

Respect for the spiritual significance of marriage is also crucial. Envisioning marriage as a partnership with God defines the relationship as a sacred union, grace-filled and strengthened by the wisdom of our Creator.

Let's Think

Do we each take enough individual responsibility for making our relationship a success?

Let's Talk

What is the best way for us to resolve our differences?

Let's Do

Let's establish our anniversary as a traditional family holiday. Let's make plans to celebrate it in a special way — perhaps with the renewal of our vows followed by a celebration with our families and friends or just the two of us.

Let's Pray

Lord, whenever we become too self-centered, step in. Remind us that we have a loving partner in our lives to whom we have vowed to give our time, our energy, our concern, and our support.

Teach us to be selfless and caring.

Don't let us ever forget that marriage is a partnership that demands adjustments, acceptance, tolerance, forgiveness, and generous doses of understanding and love.

Guide us, Lord, in our determination to build a strong, solid, respect-filled relationship.

Thank you, generous Lord, for the joys of our vocation.

STAYING IN LOVE

F alling in love is like fireworks exploding across the sky. It's so spectacular and exciting, in fact, that couples often get disillusioned about marriage. In the rigors of daily life, the fever of romance seems to wane.

Just because love is less intense, however, does not mean that it is no longer as deep and satisfying as it once was. It simply becomes more varied. There are times of profound romance and passion — and times of quiet and comfort. At times, in fact, it may even be dull. In marriage, love becomes more like the embers of a glowing fire rather than like the brilliant splashes of flashing fireworks.

The Flames of Romance

Of course, a glowing fire must constantly be fed with fuel to survive. Likewise in marriage: unless we steadily add logs of love and caring to our fire, it will eventually extinguish itself.

"Oh, how I miss the relationship we had before we were married," remarks Anita, married for a year and a half. "Rob was so different then. He made me feel so attractive and special. He always paid attention to what I had to say and went out of his way to compliment me and share his feelings with me. Now he rarely tells me how he feels. He doesn't tell me how much I mean to him."

Burdened by the stresses and strains of daily living, it doesn't take long for a young husband to forget to express his love for his best girl; it doesn't take long for a busy wife to forget to offer her husband those loving gestures that made courtship so playful and enjoyable. Over time, many couples become too serious about life. They begin taking each other for granted, assuming that expressions of affection are no longer significant.

"I sometimes wonder if Ruth feels that she made a mistake in marrying me," admits Alex. "Oh, deep down, I guess I do believe that she still loves me, but it would be so nice to hear her say it once in a while."

We all need reassurance; we need to hear — over and over again — that we are cherished and appreciated. We need to be held and hugged — often — for expressions of love such as these provide the confidence, security, and richness that every relationship needs.

The Thrill of Dating

"Sometimes I wish we had just kept dating instead of getting married," confesses Joan, who has just celebrated her second anniversary. "Our dates were always so much fun. Now when we go out, it's always with friends — never just the two of us."

You make a big mistake when you stop dating each other. After all, your love took root in that exciting way of relating. Your wedding day need not bring that to an end. More than ever, you need to date each other to keep the romance, mystery, and intrigue alive.

"I love going out to dinner alone with Don," says Sandy, a thirty-year-old newlywed. "When we have dinner together at home, we usually listen to the news or watch some sitcom on television. And even when the television isn't on, we seldom get involved in interesting and satisfying conversations like we do when we're out. The whole mood is just different when we go out."

Of course, you can't go back in time to the intense, ecstatic love you felt when you first fell in love. You can, however, occasionally recapture some of the wonderful emotions you felt at that time.

"I fall in love all over again with Karen when we go to Crystal Beach, an amusement park near our home," says Karen's husband, Michael. "She's like an excited little kid when we go there. I guess that's partly why I fell in love with her in the first place — for her enthusiasm and sense of fun."

Many newlyweds don't have enough money to date, but dates don't have to be expensive to be fun. An intimate picnic in the park or an afternoon spent flying a kite or walking in the woods can be as enjoyable as a fancy date.

"We don't even have to go out to have a romantic time together," adds Michael. "Sometimes we just spend an evening on our patio, sharing a beer and gazing at the stars — or we go outside when it's snowing and build a big snowman."

A pizza-by-candlelight dinner or playing an interesting game in front of the fireplace can be romantic. It doesn't matter what you do, as long as you give your time and attention to each other.

Couples who are working hard to build a life together often feel that they just don't have the time to set aside a few hours for mutual pleasure. Yet, making time for each other and having fun together is something your love affair cannot afford to be without.

The Joy of Surprise

Remembering each other with an occasional surprise is one way of showing love and appreciation. Peggy was really touched when her husband stopped at the corner store on his way home from work to pick up her favorite candy bar. A handful of wildflowers is as delightful as a dozen long-stemmed roses — perhaps more so.

Some couples invent their own special ways of expressing their love. "We write notes to each other," says Jane, who works the night shift as a nurse, while her husband works a daytime job as an engineer. "It's great to find a little love note lying on my pillow or taped to the coffee maker when Mark isn't at home to talk to me."

Falling deeply in love is easy, but staying deeply in love takes a bit of effort and ingenuity on the part of *both* partners.

Let's Think

Do we say "I love you" often and in creative ways? Do we compliment each other? Do we express our care and affection for each other by spending enough time together? Does either of us watch television to the extent that it interferes with genuine intimacy?

Let's Talk

What can we do to keep our marriage from getting boring?

Let's Do

Let's leave the television off one evening a week and take turns planning a simple, but enjoyable, evening at home.

Let's eat out more often — just the two of us — even if it's only pizza, hot dogs, or peanut-butter sandwiches in the park.

Let's set aside one day a month for a special date together.

Let's Pray

Lord, don't let us ever forget how important it is to express our love and affection for each other. It's so easy to just sit back and complacently take each other for granted.

Help us remember that we each have a responsibility to make our marriage interesting and enjoyable.

Teach us, Lord, to be affectionate, caring, and thoughtful. Show us how to express our love for each other.

Thank you, God, for the laughter we share.

ACCEPTING
YOUR DIFFERENCES

When two individuals marry, they do not automatically become one. In fact, the purpose of marriage is not to make one person out of two. In marriage, two persons simply become one couple with two different personalities, two different points of view, and usually two different ways of coping with life.

Living together compatibly requires both individuals to recognize, accept, and appreciate personal differences, and to adjust to each other's way of coping with the events in their shared life. If we all faced circumstances in exactly the same way, life would be easier — but life simply doesn't present us with easy and compatible alternatives.

Natural Differences

It's obvious — especially to men and women who live together — that there are definite male and female ways of doing things, masculine and feminine perspectives. Our gender often affects the way we cope with and respond to various circumstances.

Although there are exceptions and varying degrees of difference, men usually accept life as it is. Women, on the other hand, dissect, analyze, and attempt to find reasons for everything that happens. Men tend to value independence and self-reliance, and women give more importance to intimacy, relationships, and interdependence. Men are more action-oriented and like to interact with people on a physical plane, while women have a need to relate to people on a more psychological level. It's important for husbands and wives to recognize and accept these differences if they're to get along.

Besides gender differences, there are differences in personalities as well. Linda is a slow and deliberating — sometimes procrastinating — person who needs plenty of time to think things through before she does anything. Her husband, Brian, is a quick "act-before-you-think" person who jumps into situations with little prior thought. Brian has a positive and easygoing outlook on life; Linda has a more negative attitude that regards many ordinary circumstances as burdensome and worrisome.

Although their personalities complement each other in many situations, Brian and Linda struggle to accommodate each other's approach to life. It's an exercise in patience and compromise in which each gives a little to enjoy compatible living. Brian needs to slow down and wait until Linda weighs all the alternatives before acting upon something, but Linda has to trust her instinct and enjoy a little serendipity. Linda must struggle to react to circumstances more positively, and Brian must constantly remind himself to be more understanding when his wife worries about things he considers "no big deal."

Besides having gender and personality differences, some couples have different energy levels and biological clocks. When Jerry, a night person, is ready and eager to go out for the evening and enjoy himself, Alice, a morning person, is exhausted and ready to crawl into bed for the night.

When they were first married, Alice would get up early on weekends feeling hungry and full of energy. She would prepare a huge breakfast and expect Jerry to share it with her. Jerry, however, preferred to sleep later on weekends. When he finally crawled out of bed, he needed a generous dose of caffeine before he could even look at food or think of facing the day.

They worked it out. Alice decided to let Jerry sleep while she enjoyed her big weekend breakfast in the company of a good book. Every once in a while, for a change, she would accommodate Jerry's preferred schedule by postponing her own breakfast to enjoy a sumptuous breakfast in bed with him — after he had his usual ration of coffee. At other times, Jerry would willingly get up early and take Alice out for a huge breakfast treat. When they made plans to go out for a late evening, Jerry would do the dinner dishes while Alice took a short nap.

The Love in Compromise

Compromising is the loving exercise of negotiating until a solution can be accepted — though perhaps not favored — by both of you. As you each give a little and try to get closer to your partner's perspective, you both give up a little of your own preference and accept as much of your partner's preferences as possible. Compromise does not mean that one of you always gives up completely. Nor does it mean that one of you "wins" one time and the other "wins" the next time.

Each situation is unique, and the give-and-take in determining each solution is an ongoing process.

Consider alternative ways of dealing with life's situations and generous enough to give in occasionally to each other's method of handling things. Constantly insisting on your own way is usually a sign of immaturity.

Let's Think

Do we work for a compromise as often as possible? Do we try to understand why each other does things in a particular way?

Let's Talk

How can we become more accommodating to each other's manner of handling different situations?

Let's Do

When we disagree on how to handle a specific situation, let's take the time to explore the advantages and disadvantages of each option to see if it's possible for us to meet halfway. If we can't compromise, let's be willing to respect each other's stance.

Let's Pray

Lord, because we are two different individuals, we often react very differently to situations. Remind us to respect our differences.

Don't let either of us assume that our own way of doing something is better than our partner's. Teach us to consider generous alternatives.

Fill our hearts with kindness and generosity. Give us patience, wisdom, and understanding to develop a compatible and satisfying lifestyle.

Thank you, loving Creator, for the unique splendor of our respective personalities.

COMMUNICATING EFFECTIVELY

A lack of communication is probably the foremost cause of tension between spouses. Without an effective and consistent exchange of ideas, it's difficult for two people to understand and be sensitive to each other's needs.

Women, especially, complain about the lack of communication in their marriages. Barbara's situation will sound familiar. She eagerly looks forward to talking to her husband, John, at the end of the day. When they both arrive home, however, John usually needs time to unwind. He calls this "compatible silence." Although it's difficult for Barbara, she tries to be sensitive to John's need for silence and space. However, when she tries to talk to John later in the evening, she often finds him involved in some project or watching a favorite television program. If Barbara attempts to interrupt, John becomes annoyed.

"There's never a good time to talk," complains Barbara. "I doubt that the timing is poor. I think John just doesn't like to talk — at least not to me. It makes me feel so shut out and worthless — as if I'm not intelligent or important enough for him to want to talk to." John, who was never much of a conversationalist, is content with occasional bits of light and uninvolving conversation. He can't understand why Barbara feels as she does.

Jane and Paul had no trouble communicating when they dated each other. After several years of marriage, however, they have developed a definite communication gap. Jane complains that the range of Paul's conversation has shrunk to "Please pass the salt," "Is the laundry done?" and "What time is supper?" He no longer tries to talk about their mutual interests, feelings, and goals, as he did before they were married.

When Paul is confronted with Jane's complaints, he becomes defensive. He claims that whenever he tries to talk to Jane about something that's important to him, she shows a callous lack of interest. He also accuses Jane of being interested in talking mainly about problems.

Communication is a two-way exchange of ideas that has to be satisfying to both parties if the relationship is going to survive and deepen. There are many constraints that can put a damper on a person's willingness to communicate.

A Few Pertinent Questions

When a couple finds that they are having trouble conversing with each other, it may help if they each take the time to ask themselves a few pertinent questions to determine if either one of them is at fault — or at least partly at fault — for the impasse.

- *Do I give my spouse my full attention when he or she is talking, or do I let myself get distracted?*

- *Do I listen to and accept my partner's ideas and opinions, or do I constantly interrupt with my own?*
- *Do I talk mostly about problems and worries, or do I try to make my conversations pleasant and interesting?*
- *Do I regard conversations as opportunities for complaining and criticizing, or do I view them as opportunities for intimacy, learning, and understanding?*
- *Am I ever guilty of thinking that my partner's interests and feelings are unimportant or at least not as important as mine?*

Male and Female Differences

There are definite differences in the way men and women communicate. Husbands and wives must allow for and accept these differences if they are to communicate effectively.

A woman's need for communication ordinarily is much greater than a man's. Women are usually more skilled at communicating; communicating is a major component of a little girl's developmental years. She shares secrets with friends, analyzes events, and examines every detail of life. As she approaches adulthood, a young woman often considers an event somehow incomplete until she can talk about it and analyze it.

Women are also more detail-oriented than men. They love to delve into the intricacies of every relationship, every exchange, every event. They look for meaning and significance.

The lives of young boys, on the other hand, usually revolve around activity more than conversation. Since talking is not as important to them as action, boys generally don't develop conversational skills. As a result, many men are poor communicators and don't know it. In fact, a husband is often surprised to learn that his wife thinks their relationship is less than satisfying.

It's important for a couple to realize that a truly intimate relationship cannot exist without communication. Spouses who develop a relationship in which they consider each other "best friends" usually share their daily experiences and feelings with each other.

Key Guidelines

There are tactful ways to develop your communication skills.

Don't nag. Refrain from complaining about each other's failure to communicate. You cannot nag anyone into becoming a cooperative conversationalist. You can only find ways to generate interest in the topic at hand.

Keep your expectations low. If you're the one doing the talking, don't expect too much in return. Don't become impatient or defensive when your comments seem to be met with inattentiveness or unresponsiveness. Talk about your feelings, needs, hopes, dreams. If you can get each other accustomed to hearing such details expressed, mutual exchanges may develop.

Draw each other into the exchange. Ask leading questions: "Do you agree with Tom's opinion on the issue we were discussing last night?" "I feel disappointed about what happened yesterday. How do you feel about it?" "Do you think that Beth was right in refusing to go along with Jim's decision?"

Develop mutuality. Discuss topics that one of you has a sharp interest in. If, for example, crafts, sports, music, art, travel, gardening, or astronomy is something one of you is enthusiastic about, try to develop that individual interest into a mutual interest.

Read a book together, exercise together, cook together, follow current events together. Be open and honest with your interests and find a mutual activity that will generate conversation.

Make it a practice to share interesting or humorous newspaper and magazine articles with each other.

Arrange for conditions that promote conversation. One of the greatest obstacles to conversation is the presence of a television set that's constantly on. Get away from the TV as much as possible. Go for a walk together. Make it a habit to have dessert and coffee on the deck, in the backyard, or in your bedroom.

Develop exciting conversation starters. Guessing games often start conversations. Interesting quizzes and surveys published in magazines are also fun to share and use as introductions to conversation.

Affirm each other's efforts to improve. Praise each other for even minimal efforts toward mutuality. Compliment and encourage each other with statements such as, "I enjoyed talking to you today. You really know a lot about history" or "I liked the views you expressed about our Olympic teams. I'd really like to hear more about the problems you think they're facing."

Let's Think

Do we give each other our undivided and uninterrupted attention during conversations?

Do we feel that we are each other's best friend? Why or why not?

Does the television interfere with our being able to communicate intimately and effectively?

Let's Talk

What topics do we need to talk about? What makes discussing this topic (or topics) difficult?

If television controls too much of our time and attention, what can we do about it?

Let's Do

To practice conversing, let's occasionally take turns choosing a subject. Then let's set aside at least ten minutes to discuss the subject with each other.

Let's plan interesting topics of conversation for our lunch or dinner dates. Let's not discuss problems when we're out enjoying ourselves.

Let's Pray

We admit, Lord, that we are sometimes guilty of being more talkative with our friends than with each other. We often fail to give each other quality time and attention.

Teach us to communicate more openly with each other.

Teach us to trust. Teach us to risk being open with our deepest feelings, fears, joys, and hopes. Teach us to share our successes and our failures, our doubts, our dreams, our love.

Thank you, everlasting Word, for the many talks the two of us have shared.

DEVELOPING DIALOGUE

The amount of discourse does not accurately determine effective communication. Many couples talk to each other a great deal without deeply communicating. Because they view and approach life from two different perspectives and have different styles of talking, two persons can often misunderstand each other. They can even annoy each other. Not knowing how to speak and not knowing how to listen are the two causes of ineffective communication.

Understanding and exercising the dynamics of dialogue are the only ways to develop effective communication. Dialogue is a loving balance of speaking honestly and listening attentively. Interrupting, allowing distractions, and mentally moving ahead to formulate a response aggravate fruitful dialogue.

The "Be-attitudes" of Effective Dialogue

It is often said that dialogue is to intimacy in marriage what the circulatory system is to the body. This is true. Without engaging in earnest and regular dialogue, effective communication and satisfying intimacy are impossible. Keeping the "be-attitudes" of effective dialogue in mind will help you develop dialogue skills through the years ahead.

Be sensible. Timing is important in effective communication. It makes no sense to attempt a long and involved discussion when interruptions are inevitable or when one of you is fatigued, ill, pinched for time, or distracted by other concerns. Never discuss important issues when one of you is angry, moody, or depressed. Be willing to postpone your dialogues; postponing doesn't mean it's canceled. Make time for the exchange at the soonest sensible moment.

Be interested. Show interest in what each other is saying — even when you are not particularly interested in the topic. Your love for each other manifests itself in countless, subtle ways — and showing interest when you're not is a powerful way of saying deeply and intimately, "I love you. Your interests make me interested in you."

Be involved. Listening is not a passive exercise. Listening means becoming involved in what your spouse is saying. When you're listening, focus your attention on what you're hearing. To reassure yourself and your spouse that you are, in fact, *hearing* what is being said, paraphrase what your spouse tells you: "What I hear you saying is that you don't really think I'm handling this problem in the best possible manner." This form of involved listening safeguards meaning.

Be sensitive. Listen with an open mind. Try to see each other's point of view. Opinions, feelings, dreams, and fears are not right or wrong. They simply reflect an individual's perception of the world. To quip that an opinion is stupid or a fear is dumb is to discount the very personhood of your lover.

At times, paying attention to each other's words isn't enough, though. Feelings and moods often hide behind words. As you listen, try to determine how your spouse feels at the moment. Don't assume, however, that you know. Ask for verification: "Are you feeling insecure about this?" "Are you angry?" "Are you pleased with the results?"

Be objective. There are many ways of looking at every situation and many possible solutions to conflicts and tensions. Unless specifically asked for, the object of dialogue is not to seek advice. Being judgmental and offering advice inhibit the free-flowing potential of dialogue.

Be specific. Define the issue at hand and stick to it. Give enough detail to clarify the situation without frustrating the exchange.

Be positive. Unpleasant issues have to be discussed. Discussing unpleasantries, however, doesn't mean the atmosphere has to be strained with irritation, negative thinking, and judgmentalism. Maintain a positive and hopeful atmosphere for your dialogues.

Be gracious. Honor each other's viewpoints and concerns. Do not become argumentative or critical. Do not offer contradictory viewpoints in a manner that negates each other's position. Ask "What do you think about this way of looking at things?" This kind of inquiry keeps the exchange gracious, respectful, productive, and loving.

Be trustworthy. The intimacy and friendship nurtured in dialogue is like sacred lovemaking. It requires the same naked trust and comfort that physical intimacy entails. Respect standards of confidentiality. Dialogue is impossible without integrity.

With courtesy, patience, objectivity, integrity, and a passionate and genuine interest in each other, you can fine-tune your dialogue techniques. Effective communication and satisfying intimacy are the results.

Let's Think

Do we blame each other when we have trouble communicating? Do we try to be objective as we listen to each other?

Let's Talk

How do we annoy each other? What can we do about these annoying behaviors?

How well do we dialogue?

Let's Do

Let's find some reading material on marital communication and read it together.

Let's Pray

Teach us, Lord, to communicate in ways that draw us closer together. Teach us to be kind, available, patient, open-minded, accepting, and understanding. Let us realize that only through strong dialogue will we communicate effectively and come to appreciate each other with fidelity and reverence.

Thank you, Lord, for the deep friendship we share.

HANDLING THE GIVE-AND-TAKE OF MARRIAGE

Does a perfect fifty-fifty relationship in marriage actually exist? Ask any long-married couple. They will probably agree that the give-and-take of marriage is seldom — if ever — perfectly or constantly equal. There are times when one partner must be willing to carry a heavier percentage.

Charles and Joyce, two dedicated career persons, were determined to have a perfectly equal partnership: a well-balanced fifty-fifty relationship. As a result, they became acutely aware of what each other was contributing to their marriage in both time and energy. When one felt the other was failing to give an adequate amount to the relationship, the complaining would begin. Finally, Charles and Joyce actually started to keep track of all the little favors they did for each other.

One morning after a particularly heated argument about

whose turn it was to make the morning coffee, the couple realized that their scorekeeping was ridiculous. "It was ruining our relationship," Charles admits. Constantly measuring their marital debits and credits had created a wall of resentment between them.

"It took us about six months of bickering," Joyce confesses, "to realize that marriage is not based on a scorekeeping system. We decided to confine our scorekeeping exercises to card games and golf."

Achieving a Balance

Balance in a relationship is possible if both partners will give whatever it takes to make the other's life easier and better.

Joan and Carl have been married for twenty years. They feel they've achieved a balance simply by being considerate of each other's welfare. When they were first married, Joan had a part-time job, did all the housework, shopped, and gardened. Her taking on these responsibilities left Carl free to build up a failing insurance business he inherited from his father. When business improved and the couple had children, Carl took on some of the extra financial and household responsibilities.

There were times, however, when Carl's work schedule was so demanding that Joan lowered her expectations. There was also a time when Joan's determination to finish her college education led Carl to pitch in as much as he could to make it easier for her.

It worked this way with the various problems and stresses in their lives. There were a couple of years when caring for her ailing parent taxed Joan's stress level. During that time, Carl went out of his way to lend her his support. There were times when Carl's business problems caused him so much anxiety that Joan made it a point to set her own worries aside to help alleviate his.

The give-and-take in this marriage never caused concern. Although it was seldom equal, Joan and Carl managed to balance their day-to-day relationship with love, consideration, and appreciation for each other.

Changing the Formula

The most successful marriages discard the fifty-fifty understanding and adopt a one hundred-one hundred understanding. Both spouses give one hundred percent of their love, concern, energy, talents, and total selves to the relationship. Couples in one hundred-one hundred relationships give *and* receive one hundred percent!

Let's Think

Do we give our marriage enough time, energy, and concern?

Do we expect too much of each other? Do we expect enough from ourselves?

Let's Talk

How and what do we each contribute to our relationship? In what areas can we each improve our giving?

How do we receive from each other? Are we grateful and courteous without thinking, "Now what do I have to do to balance this out"?

Let's Do

Let's express our appreciation for the things we do for each other. Let's be more considerate of each other.

Let's Pray

Lord, let us mature in our relationship. Help us refrain from keeping score of what each of us contributes to our marriage.

Let us always be willing to give one hundred percent of our dedication, involvement, concern, and love to our relationship.

Help us remember, Lord, to be fair.

Help us make each other's lives as peaceful and satisfying as possible. Help us remember Jesus' model of coming to serve rather than being served.

Thank you, gracious God, for the little things that make life sweet.

ACCEPTING EACH OTHER'S FAULTS

A marriage license does not give a person the right or the responsibility to change his or her partner. The marriage vows make a statement of acceptance, for better or for worse, warts and all.

Before marriage, couples have little trouble accepting each other. The eyes of love have a tendency to blind a person to the beloved's faults. Shortly into marriage, however, they begin to see their "perfect partner" turn into a real person with the usual allotment of human faults and frailties. Crabby morning dispositions, toothpaste-smeared mirrors, and casually discarded clothing are the makings of real people.

From Perfect Partners to Real People

A few weeks after she returned from her honeymoon, Ann acknowledged that her new husband was annoyingly short-tempered. She had seen displays of his temper while they were dating, but his anger was never directed at her. Because the outbursts were short-lived and nonviolent, Ann had overlooked them.

Gradually, Ann became more and more aware of how disruptive and disturbing her husband's temper could be. She became determined to change him into a calmer and gentler person.

Ann tried everything from responding calmly and lovingly to her husband's outbursts to getting angry and fighting back. Nothing worked. No matter how she tried, Ann could not bring about a change in her husband's behavior.

Eventually, Ann realized that her husband was the type of person who simply had to get his anger and frustrations out or he couldn't function. This was a part of her spouse that she would have to live with if their marriage was to be satisfying. She had managed to overlook the outbursts before they were married. She could teach herself to overlook them now.

Ann's determination led her to concentrate more on her husband's virtues: his kindness, his sense of responsibility, and his sensitivity to her feelings. Ann realized that these strengths far outweighed his occasional outbursts.

After five years of marriage, Ann failed to change her spouse. The only thing she managed to change was her own attitude toward his faults. She learned that the only person she could change was herself; she could change no one else.

Befriending the Imperfections

It is possible to accept and overlook each other's faults. In fact, many long-married couples believe you can come to view your beloved's faults with a certain amount of affection.

"I remember how annoyed I used to get with Harry when we were first married," Stefanie reminisces after twenty-four years of marriage. "He was the type of person who never put anything away. He left his jackets and sweaters lying on chairs. When he did a home-repair job, he'd leave his tools scattered on the garage floor. Everything he ever touched was left either uncapped, uncovered, unhung, or unreplaced. He's still that way." Stefanie remembers the arguments and Harry's many futile attempts to be neater.

After years of promises and failures, Stefanie began to regard Harry as a person who possessed an unexplainable — but forgivable — mental block against putting things away. She realized that Harry's messiness was not an intentional plot to annoy her. He was simply engrossed in other things. Ann eventually grew to regard Harry's absent-mindedness as an endearing trait — as well as an annoyance.

"Someone once told me," Ann concludes, "that when you learn how to love your spouse's faults, you can finally consider yourselves truly in love."

Let's Think

Do we criticize each other's faults in ways that are constructive or loving?

Do we tend to think that our own faults are less annoying?

Let's Talk

How do we point out each other's faults?
How often do we compliment each other?

Let's Do

Let's put extra effort into expressing appreciation for each other. Let's be as specific as possible.

Let's Pray

Lord, it's easy to forget that we're not perfect — especially when we're expecting perfection from each other.

Teach us, Lord, to focus on each other's strengths and virtues. Lead us to see beyond each other's faults.

Teach us, Lord, how to accept and love each other just as we are.

Thank you, almighty Creator, for the imperfections in each of us.

LEARNING
TO DISAGREE

Two individuals living together day in and day out will inevitably disagree. Married couples should expect to argue. In fact, they should expect some serious battles in which full measures of anger and frustration are vented. Hurt feelings may even result. Couples should also expect apologies, forgiveness, and a deeper sense of intimacy to follow such arguments.

Alan and Nancy believed that arguing indicated a marriage was falling apart. They had gotten along well during their courtship and assumed that meant they were comfortably compatible. They didn't expect to fight. In fact, they were actually afraid to fight.

"We thought that fighting would eventually destroy our relationship," observes Nancy. "But the more we avoided arguing, the more resentment built up between us. One day when we finally exploded, we were surprised at how relieved we felt. It felt so good to get some of those resentments out in the open. We had no trouble apologizing and forgiving each other — and, oh, how wonderful it was to make up!"

The Benefits of Arguing

An argument is not just a fight; it's a viewing and ventilating of differences. When we argue, differences that are often held inside and allowed to fester are brought into the open where they can be examined and dealt with. This process promotes a better understanding of each other's views. It leads to a meeting of minds on divergent views. Rather than acting as a wedge between spouses, arguments can bring couples closer together in a more understanding relationship.

Arguments also get rid of moodiness. We often become crabby and sulky when we're not given the opportunity to discuss and resolve our differences. There are times when sulking and pouting do a lot more damage than fighting does.

During the first few months of their marriage, John and Lauren refused to fight with each other. "When I'd get upset about something," Lauren explains, "I'd tell John off. But instead of fighting back, he would just go off and sulk. And that would make me twice as angry. I felt cheated; I didn't get to express my views and I didn't get to hear his. I would get totally frustrated and remain angry for days."

Lauren finally realized why John refused to fight: for years, he had listened to his parents' hostile bickering. He assumed that fighting was damaging to a marriage. When Lauren assured John that an occasional disagreement wouldn't destroy her love for him, he became less hesitant about arguing.

Of course, any argument can become ugly and damaging. To avoid excessive and prolonged bitterness, learn how to fight fairly.

Key Guidelines

Disagreements need not be destructive. The following suggestions can keep your disagreements reasonable — even constructive.

Avoid a battlefront mentality. Your arguments are not battles that have to be won. Entering into an argument with a battlefront mentality only leaves two losers. Arguing with the intentions to understand each other and resolve the conflict assures a loving — albeit heated — exchange that holds the potential of being productive.

Avoid feeling absolutely right. Few arguments involve one person who is totally right and one who is totally wrong. Most disagreements contain views and opinions that are valid from more than one perspective. Both deserve equal respect, thought, and consideration. If you begin to feel that you are absolutely right on an issue, inventory your attitude. You may be harboring a battlefront mentality.

Avoid shouting matches. One of the most unfair — and perhaps most childish — ways to argue is the shouting match. The chaos of a shouting match can lead to name-calling, exaggerations, falsehoods, and irrational behavior. Allow each other's opinions to be stated calmly and completely. "Andy has such a loud voice," complains Marie, "that he can easily outshout me. When he starts shouting, he completely drowns me out. I get frustrated and angry. I try to scream back at him and end up crying so hard I can hardly talk." Andy's unfair tactics undermine any opportunity for him and Marie to settle their differences. They can't even learn what the differences are.

Listen with calm objectivity. To achieve a good under-standing of your differences, listen with a calm and open mind. View each other's opinions with utmost respect. Try to put yourselves in each other's shoes. The more you respect each other's view, the better chance you have of under-standing each other on a more intimate level. With such objectivity, your arguing can be more logical and productive.

Don't resurrect old arguments. "Whenever we start argu-ing," says Tom, "Janet brings up stuff that has bothered her in the past. Before you know it, we're arguing about issues I thought were settled a long time ago." Resurrecting former disagreements never helps settle a current argument. It mere-ly makes each party angrier and more argumentative. Stick to the issues at hand.

Avoid generalizations. Generalizations excite confusion, defensiveness, and more anger. "You *always...*" or "You *never...*" doesn't take an exchange in a positive direction.

Give each other the benefit of the doubt. Jumping to unfair conclusions and pinning nonexistent motives on each other leave your relationship with very little — if any — integrity.

When your emotions begin to intensify, call a truce; take a breather. It's impossible to argue logically when anger interferes with reasoning. Take time to cool down before trying to settle a disagreement.

Compromise. When you find your viewpoints so far apart that agreeing seems impossible, love each other enough to compromise. (Review page 19-20.) Examine your positions, brainstorm for other options, and find a middle ground.

If a compromise is not possible, quit! Don't force the

issue. Bring the discussion to a respectful close, agreeing to disagree.

Admit to error. Be willing to admit to your own short-sightedness or misunderstanding. If during a disagreement you suddenly realize that you've overlooked a crucial point or misunderstood a significant fact, lovingly apologize. An unwillingness to admit to error is a sign of immaturity and insecurity.

Welcome humor. See the insignificance of some of your differences. A good laugh in the middle of an argument can dispel anger and inspire both of you to admit that you may be partly wrong. An unexpected hug usually helps, too.

Forgive. Jesus manifested a compassionate and merciful God. A covenant such as your marriage calls for the compassion, mercy, and forgiveness Jesus taught.

Let's Think

Are we fair when we disagree with each other? Do we take advantage of each other's anger and frustration?

Do we assume that we're both a little bit right and a little bit wrong?

Do we bring up old arguments?

Let's Talk

What can we do to better understand each other's opinions?

What words, phrases, or behaviors make our arguments damaging instead of productive?

How can we best express forgiveness?

Let's Do

When either of us realizes that an argument is getting out of hand, let's give each other a prearranged signal such as a raised right hand or a "cut" sign. Let's immediately stop arguing, take ten minutes to cool off, and then try again.

Let's Pray

Lord, teach us how to approach disagreements with minds that are open to each other's opinions. Make our hearts sensitive to each other's feelings.

Teach us to resolve our differences with a sense of fairness, a sense of humor, and an abundance of love.

When we disagree, help us remember to strive for a resolution rather than a victory. Teach us to disagree agreeably.

Thank you, Lord, for the trust we share.

APOLOGIZING AND FORGIVING

Apologizing and forgiving play key roles in a couple's honesty and intimacy. Most long-married couples disagree with the popular slogan, "Love means never having to say you're sorry." In fact, the longer a couple is married, the more willing they are to apologize and forgive.

Apologizing and forgiving are as important to a relationship as eating and sleeping are to living. Some people, however, find it extremely difficult to apologize.

When Kathy and Andrew fight, Andrew usually apologizes first — not because he's ordinarily the one who's wrong. Rather, Andrew simply finds apologizing easier to do than Kathy does. Kathy, who is more easily hurt than Andrew, is likely to spend more time nursing her wounded feelings and sulking.

Kathy's concentration on her offended feelings often results in pent-up resentment. On the other hand, Andrew's willingness to apologize usually defuses bitter feelings and prevents major damage to their relationship.

Couples have the choice of forgiving quickly or allowing resentments to fester inside. The more time they give their resentments to build, the bigger the barrier they erect between themselves. Eventually, this barrier will become too large and too difficult for them to tear down.

Sincere and speedy apologies are necessary if a couple is to maintain a solid and healthy relationship. In turn, apologies must be accepted and forgiveness exercised.

The Partnership of Apologizing and Forgiving

Apologizing and forgiving form a partnership in a strong marriage. The details of who apologizes and who forgives are irrelevant, but one does not genuinely exist without the other. An apology is extended with confidence that forgiveness is imminent. Forgiveness is offered, readily and unconditionally, as the natural and faithful response to an apology.

Ted hates to apologize. "It's not that Carol means to be unforgiving. She's willing to accept my apology and forgive. But she needs to analyze our arguments after they're finished — and before you know it, we're at it again."

There's danger in trying to assess exactly who was right or who was wrong, who is to blame and who is blameless. Keeping score of who started an argument, who was right, who apologized first, or who did the forgiving inhibits a couple's ability to honestly apologize and forgive. An analysis of blame accomplishes little more than triggering another argument.

When Apologizing Is Difficult

Apologizing is often difficult. If you can't apologize for being wrong or for misunderstanding each other, apologize for having hurt each other. If you find it difficult to say "I'm sorry. I was wrong," say "I'm sorry I hurt you" or "I'm sorry I made you angry."

Sometimes it's easier for the person who is least wrong to apologize first. This leads to a strong measure of mutuality. Once an "I'm sorry" has been extended, "I'm sorry, too" is often forthcoming.

A simple, loving gesture often says more than apologetic words. An unexpected hug, the offer of a cup of coffee, an affectionate note, or a simple phone call from work will often bring an end to offended feelings.

When Forgiving Is Difficult

Deep wounds make forgiving difficult. Our natural tendencies toward self-pity, self-righteousness, and anger obstruct forgiveness. "It's not fair for my spouse to hurt me so deeply and then to think that a handful of words is going to make everything just fine."

Forgiveness becomes especially difficult when one of you has ultimately and undeniably been "proven right." Those nasty little words "I told you so" churn within and scream for expression. Genuine forgiveness, however, cannot align with an I-told-you-so attitude.

No one is perfect, and loving couples realize this. Tempers flare, words are said, and feelings get hurt. This is part of intimate relating. The grace of your sacrament blesses you with the gift to forgive with divine forgiveness. After all, forgiveness isn't a feeling; it's an act. Forgiving each other, graciously and gracefully, respects and celebrates the reality of your covenant.

Let's Think

Do we admit when we're wrong? Are we quick and gracious about extending apologies? Are we quick and gracious in accepting apologies?

Let's Talk

How can we help each other to apologize quickly?
What forms of apology are the most meaningful for us?

Let's Do

If we haven't apologized by the end of the day, let's hug and apologize before we go to bed.

If we have trouble saying "I'm sorry," let's write our apologies or express contrition in some small gesture.

Let's Pray

Lord, we sometimes stubbornly hang on to our anger and resentment. We blame each other for our disagreements.

Teach us, Lord, to be more forgiving and understanding.

Take away our destructive and vengeful feelings. Show us how to be kind and humble. Help us dispose of bitterness and embrace contrition and forgiveness.

Lord, give us the wisdom and the love we need to apologize quickly and forgive completely.

Thank you, merciful God, for your unconditional love.

HANDLING
JEALOUSY

Jealousy in marriage is like a cancer. It quietly eats away at trust and blocks intimacy. It kills spontaneity, breeds competition, and limits mutuality.

"Rick really upsets and embarrasses me at times," complains Mona, a newlywed of seven months. "I knew he was a flirt before I married him, but I thought he would change once we were married. Yet, whenever we're at a party, he flirts with half the women there."

Mona considers Rick's flirting totally inappropriate and feels justified in complaining about it. Rick, on the other hand, doesn't understand Mona's resentment. He's faithful and trustworthy. He sees his flirting as nothing more than friendly socializing.

Inward Jealousy

Inward jealousy begins with a person's orientation toward his or her spouse. Rick fails to recognize the effect his behavior has on his spouse. He fails to recognize the fine line between being friendly and being provocative. People who defend Rick's manner of socializing should ask themselves the following questions. Perhaps such behavior is, indeed, inappropriate.

- *Do the people with whom I flirt realize that my intention is merely to be friendly?*
- *When I'm at a social event, does my friendliness exceed that of other guests?*
- *Does my friendly socializing cause tension in my marriage?*
- *At parties, do I spend too little time with my spouse?*

Granted, some people are overly sensitive to their partner's friendly relationships with others. A spouse who is innocently outgoing and affectionate should not be subjected to an obsessive and unfair lack of trust.

Jealousy, accusations, and distrust do not promote fidelity. A couple nurtures fidelity and confidence by being sensitive to each other's feelings, by being genuinely concerned about and interested in each other's needs, and by openly showing love, affection, and respect for each other.

Outward Jealousy

Jealousy can be directed toward people and circumstances outside the marriage. The results are still damaging to the relationship.

Carla and Ray had serious problems with jealousy in the first few years of their marriage. They were both immature and insecure people who were extremely dissatisfied with the way their lives were going.

Carla worked the evening shift at an understaffed hospital. She was dissatisfied with her job and missed spending evenings with her husband. Ray had a nine-to-five office job and enjoyed his evenings with family and friends. Carla sharply resented the limitations her work schedule placed on her social time.

Ray, a self-centered person, showed little sympathy for Carla's dissatisfaction. He had his own disappointments with life. He felt his salary was not a just wage, he was jealous of his friends' more prestigious positions, and he resented his economic limitations. He could not afford the nice homes, cars, and leisure opportunities his friends enjoyed. Because of these disappointments and frustrations, Ray was hard to live with.

Ray's and Carla's envy was fed from sources outside their relationship. So was Donna's. She was jealous of her friends' marriages. She would compare her own marriage with the relationships she observed her married friends enjoying. The contrast was depressing. Donna saw her friends enjoying affection, intimacy, and friendship in their marriages — characteristics she felt were missing from her own marriage. She believed that most of her friends had husbands who were more sensitive, more talkative, and more romantic than her husband. As a result, she often nagged her spouse to be more attentive. Her attitude and behavior put a great strain on their marriage.

Carla, Ray, and Donna were victims of their own envious natures. Their relationships suffered because of the attitudes they themselves chose to nurture and develop.

We are free to chose the attitudes with which we wish to face life. We can develop positive, uplifting attitudes, which ordinarily lead to contentment, or negative, destructive attitudes, which bring frustration and unhappiness.

Many of us fail to realize that our own chosen attitudes toward life determine our happiness. If circumstances determine our happiness, then healthy and wealthy people, who can afford to do and have anything they want, would be automatically happy. Yet, this is seldom the case. It should also follow that those who endure difficult financial problems or disastrous health problems should be unhappy. Yet, we all know people who, despite such problems, find deep and abiding peace and contentment.

Choose Jealousy-free Relating

Learn to accept life as it is — which is neither fair nor easy. Life is only as good and as satisfying as you choose to make it. It is up to you to choose satisfaction or discontent.

If you choose to face life with envy, greed, and distrust, you choose discontent. If you choose faith, freedom, and trust, you choose the life in abundance that Jesus promises.

Let's Think

Are we basically satisfied and content with our relationship or do we struggle with inward or outward jealousy?

Is our fidelity to each other evident in social and work environments?

Let's Talk

What do we do that makes a statement about our fidelity to each other?

Do we both have a positive attitude toward life?

Let's Do

Let's make a list of our blessings and refer to it whenever either of us becomes jealous and dissatisfied with what we have or with the way our lives are going.

Let's develop a sign we can give each other in social settings when either of us feels we're being ignored.

Let's openly and maturely discuss our jealousies and insecurities rather than pouting about them.

Let's Pray

Let us realize, Lord, how destructive envy can be. Teach us to handle jealousy in ways that deepen our intimacy and fidelity.

Support us in our attempts to be sensitive to each other, to reassure each other, to help each other put to rest disturbing jealousies.

Bless us with the wisdom to develop healthy attitudes toward life, attitudes that foster contentment, satisfaction, and fulfillment.

And don't let us ever forget, Lord, that our life and our marriage will be only as happy and as satisfying as we are willing and determined to make it.

Thank you, God, for your abiding peace.

DEVELOPING
SENSITIVITY

D ebra complains that her husband, Frank, never sympa-
thizes with — or even notices — how she feels, especially when she's feeling discouraged or worried. She
thinks he's extremely insensitive and lacking in understanding.

Frank, on the other hand, thinks Debra's complaints are
unfair. "Debra would prefer to sulk than say what's bothering
her. Why doesn't she just come out and say that she's worried
or discouraged or angry or whatever?"

"We've been married for two years," Debra observes.
"Frank should know me well enough to realize what I'm
feeling without my having to tell him."

Debra's thinking is not mature or fair. She relates intimacy
with mind reading. She completely ignores the fact that
Frank's personality is different. She overlooks the fact that
his gender gives him a different perspective. Because of these
differences, Frank will not react the same as Debra. Being
married to Debra does not automatically give Frank the
ability to know what she thinks, feels, and needs.

Debra worries about problems and details, problems and details Frank scarcely notices. Debra is afraid of certain possibilities that Frank considers insignificant. Because their approaches to life are dramatically different, they need to let each other know what's going on in their minds and hearts. "I feel angry about this" and "I'm really worried about that" are loving exchanges between a couple investing in a shared life.

Sensitivity Is Essential

We're all different — thus, expressing and explaining our feelings are essential in developing a genuine and intimate sensitivity toward others.

Most women are vocal about their feelings and can't understand why their husbands keep their feelings locked inside. Women don't mind talking about their faults and mistakes; they feel more human and accessible when they can discuss their weaknesses. Men, on the other hand, shy away from discussing the depths of their fears, concerns, and dreams. The risk of vulnerability seems like a major threat. They feel less manly and self-reliant if they expose intimate parts of themselves. These major differences call for sensitivity on both sides.

Key Guidelines

Developing a genuine sensitivity for each other is not an overnight process. It takes time, patience, and an invested interest in the overall well-being of your marriage.

Listen to each other. Notice facial expressions, body language, and voice intonations. Becoming sensitive to each other involves total attention and total listening.

Stand in each other's shoes. See and feel things from each other's point of view. Your natural temperament, gender, family background, and life experiences mold you. As a result, you react differently to all of life. Stand in each other's shoes and try to envision how things must look and feel. Check this out with each other: "Are you afraid?" "Are you excited?" "Are you sad?" "How are you feeling about the way things are right now?"

Honor each other's feelings. Feelings are neither right nor wrong. You cannot control them, in yourselves or others — and they are not to be judged. It doesn't matter if the feeling is appropriate or inappropriate, understandable or illogical. It's real and valid, and it's a vital part of who you are at the moment. "You don't really feel that way" is a statement that rips away at the integrity of your intimacy. Do not deny each other the dignity of respecting each other's feelings.

Affirm each other's feelings. Affirming each other's feelings involves acknowledgment. Show your acceptance and confirmation of each other's feelings with comments like "I understand how you feel and I feel bad for you" or "I've never experienced what you have. Tell me what you're feeling so I can better understand."

Respect each other's feelings. Since feelings are neither right nor wrong, do not criticize each other's feelings. When Paul tried to tell Marie about how angry he was with his boss, Marie was openly critical. She had her own ideas about the conflict and criticized Paul for the way he was handling it. Her criticism did not respect Paul's anger. In fact, it only served to make him more hesitant about sharing concerns in the future.

Be willing to take the initiative. Some people are uncomfortable expressing their feelings. It's not that they're afraid of criticism; it's not that they intend to withdraw or be secretive. They are afraid of becoming vulnerable — or they simply don't know *how* to express themselves.

Be willing to take the initiative when expressing feelings. Be willing to say, for example, "I felt very pleased about what happened last night. How did you feel about it?" or "Do you feel as angry as I do about Jack's refusal to cooperate?"

Conditioning Yourselves to Be Sensitive

When feelings are strong, they can actually blind you to the fact that others might feel differently. Use the less intense issues to become aware of this. When you differ — but not dramatically — use that opportunity to be gentle and sensitive to each other's feelings. Then, when the two of you differ seriously, you will be better equipped to exercise sensitivity. It's like flexing muscles so they'll be strong when you need them.

Let's Think

Do we share our true feelings with each other? Are we comfortable letting each other see our weaknesses, fears, and shortcomings? If not, why?

Let's Talk

What interferes with our being able to share our feelings freely?

What can we do to help each other become comfortable sharing on a deeper level?

Let's Do

When we seem to be misunderstanding each other's feelings, let's sit down and give each other the chance to be more precise.

Let's arrange for an occasional "sensitivity date." Let's take a picnic to the park or have a special candlelight dinner and talk specifically about our feelings.

Let's Pray

There are times, Lord, when we become so absorbed in our own interests and desires that we become unaware of each other's needs. There are times when we even fail to see each other's hurt, discouragement, fear, or excitement.

Lord, teach us to be more thoughtful and considerate. Touch us with a sweet awareness of each other's needs.

Endow us with the grace to reach out to each other with tenderness and respect, to feel each other's pain and offer comfort, to recognize each other's problems and offer support, to perceive each other's doubts and offer encouragement, to be aware of each other's need for love and respond selflessly.

Thank you, Lord, for the splendid mystery of our human nature.

Getting Through
a Bad Day

Tom and Angela ordinarily get along well. At times, however, they have a bad day and take their frustrations out on each other.

"Last Saturday was a nightmare," explains Angela. "Tom was in a terrible mood. He just picked-picked-picked the entire day. Nothing I did satisfied him.

"At first, I tried to ignore his crabbiness. Then, when he criticized the dinner I took two hours to prepare, I really blew up. We had a terrible argument and ate our dinner in silence.

"Later that evening, Tom told me that he'd had an argument with his supervisor at work the day before — and that was what had put him in such a foul mood."

When we're in the midst of acting out our frustrations, a little voice deep inside says, "This is not fair to those I love." Yet, we are emotional human beings and often use those who are closest and most precious to us as punching bags for our frustrated emotions.

We sometimes get into arguments with our partners, not

because of something they said or did, but because we feel vengeful and frustrated. We become totally egocentric and want to have someone else feel as bad as we do.

Claiming Responsibility

When you catch yourselves dumping your crabbiness on each other, be honest enough to admit it. Claim responsibility for your own mood. Recognize the injustice and immaturity in aiming your frustrations at another. Don't insist that others suffer because you're suffering. Tom could have refrained from riling up Angela's anger if he had explained the argument he'd had with his boss.

Your marriage will see good days and bad days — highs and lows. Circumstances usually determine these good days and bad days — circumstances that are much beyond your control. Some days will sparkle with harmony and accord, the two of you will be in tune with each other, and life will have a certain sweet rhythm to it. Some days will drag with tension, nothing will seem organized or synchronized, and there will be no harmony or accord between the two of you.

On days such as this, just stay out of each other's way. Make an announcement to that effect: "I happen to be crabby today. Give me lots of space, and I'll talk later." Just a simple statement such as "I'm feeling really frustrated and crabby today, Honey, and it isn't your fault" is enough to ward off an angry confrontation.

Key Guidelines

Don't let the bad days threaten your overall enjoyment of life together. There are key guidelines to help you get through the bad days on your way to the good ones.

Remain available to each other. There may be times when one of you is blinded by frustration. The one who is more emotionally stable at the time has the responsibility to remain patiently and peacefully available to the other. The best way to express this stable availability is to comment on the frustration and offer acceptance: "You seem upset about something today. Is there anything I can help you with?" or "I know something's bothering you. If you want to talk about it, I'd be glad to listen."

Don't offer advice; don't ask for it. When lending a sympathetic ear to your spouse on a bad day, avoid offering advice. When you're the one having the bad day, don't ask for advice. It's hard to accept advice, even good advice, when frustration abounds. Just be present for each other, ready to listen, ready to be honest about your frustrations, ready to take responsibility.

Avoid fatalistic thinking. Don't let the bad days define life for you. Even when there seem to be more bad days than good during a given stretch of time, remember the mystery of your faith. There must be Holy Saturday time to enter into the radiant joy of Easter.

Review the bad days. Don't let the bad days go by without some kind of review. In the event that both of you happen to be having a bad day at the same time, agree to talk about it immediately — or to postpone the exchange until you can be more optimistic. But don't let the experience escape without some discussion of what the tension was about. Examining a bad day sheds light on the next one — not to mention the humor you can often find in the midst of it all.

Mutual sympathy, patience, understanding, and a sense of

humor go a lot further in weathering a stormy day than do silence, sulkiness, and self-pity.

Let's Think

Are we fair and mature in expressing our frustrations to each other? Do we take our frustrations out on each other?

Do we recognize those times when we've given each other valid reasons to be angry or frustrated? Do we respond with patience, forbearance, contrition, and forgiveness?

Let's Talk

How can we best deal with our bad days?

What's the best approach for discussing our frustrations during a bad day?

Let's Do

On those days when we just can't seem to get along, let's give each other a hug and call a truce. Let's try to discover and understand what's really bothering us.

Let's Pray

Lord, there are days when we get unreasonably crabby and short-tempered with each other. Help us realize how unfair it is for us to dump our crabbiness on each other.

Grant us, Lord, the ability to be nice to each other, even when we don't especially feel like being nice. Teach us to work out our frustrations in mature and less hurtful ways. Teach us to respond to each other's occasional bad moods with patience, understanding, and great love.

Thank you, sweet Lord, for your abundant grace.

CRITICIZING WITH LOVE

Being exposed to our spouse's faults day after day can cause us to become overly critical. Yet, married life would be much sweeter if we'd stop looking for halos over each other's heads. We're all human — very human. We are capable of deep discernment and wisdom, and we're capable of shortsightedness and recklessness.

Because of this, we all need a bit of critical advice now and then. We need constructive criticism and loving direction.

Kim is married to a man twelve years her senior. Her husband's determination to change Kim into a more mature and sophisticated woman has resulted in an unfair amount of daily criticism. No matter what Kim does, her husband advises her on how to do it better. "He doesn't intend to be mean or degrading," Kim admits. "In fact, he thinks he's being supportive and encouraging, but he's not. The constant criticism chips away at my self-confidence. Sometimes I feel completely stupid and worthless."

Constructive Criticism

Being imperfect ourselves, we have no right to expect perfection from others. Any attempt to goad another toward perfection through criticism is hurtful and insulting. It strips away self-esteem.

Critical advice should be given sparingly. It should also be given tactfully, lovingly, and without any trace of smugness or self-righteousness.

Constructive criticism is free of judgment and anger. It respects the marvelous individuality of others and is directed toward their good. Paul's words about love in 1 Corinthians 13 could be paraphrased to say the same thing about criticism: "Loving criticism is patient and kind; it is never rude and never seeks its own advantage. It does not rejoice at wrongdoing. It is always ready to make allowances."

Key Guidelines

There are ways to give and receive critical advice without offending or angering each other.

Criticize the action, not the person. It's much better to say, "Honey, I don't feel that the way you're handling this problem is really the best way to do it" rather than "You're sure being stupid and stubborn about this?"

Limit criticisms to the immediate problem. When offering critical advice, avoid blanket statements such as "Why do you always mess things up like that?" or "Why is it you never clean up after yourself?" Such generalized accusations allow anger a foothold. Limit criticisms to the specific problem that exists at a particular moment.

Acknowledge your own imperfections. Criticism is less offensive if you include your own shortcomings in the exchange. "I think both of us should try to remember to shut the lights off" rather than "Why can't you ever remember to shut the lights off?" gives the responsibility — and the failure to be responsible — to both of you.

Honestly accentuate the positive. A positive critical comment is easier to accept than a blunt negative criticism. For example, "I love the way you look in your navy pinstriped suit. I don't think you wear anything that becomes you more" delivers a much more positive message than "I hate the way you look in that old gray suit. Wear the navy one instead."

Soften criticism with praise. By mixing criticism with praise, you affirm rather than offend. "You're such a big help with the dishes, Honey, and I really appreciate it. But I wish you wouldn't leave greasy dishes soaking in cold water." A caution is in order here: be honest with your praise. Do not fabricate something positive; that leads to manipulation.

Keep your criticisms private. Criticizing with an audience is demeaning. It eats away at trust and integrity, the cornerstones to your intimacy. It damages your relationship and communicates to others a great deal about what your marriage is — and is not.

Remain humble and objective. A common and annoying way to respond to critical advice is to counter it with criticism of your own. For many people, in fact, countercriticism is a reflex action. Countercriticism and defensiveness, however, generate anger, which leads to futile arguing. Humility and objectivity leave you open to growth, learning, and wisdom. Don't deprive each other of these virtues. Admit your imperfections without becoming defensive.

The Honesty Ingredient

Honesty is an important ingredient in any marriage. There's a point at which honesty, when it's associated with criticism, however, can be overdone.

You can determine the amount of honesty that's acceptable in a given situation by asking yourself the following questions:

- *Is what I'm about to say going to hurt my beloved's feelings?*
- *Will my observations and comments do more harm than good?*
- *Will my criticism damage my spouse's self-esteem?*
- *Is my criticism directed toward the good of my partner or am I building up my own ego?*

Honest criticism will be much more effective if we soften it with kindness.

Let's Think

Do we understand our own motives when we criticize each other? Do we criticize appropriately, or do we expect too much of each other? Do we graciously accept constructive criticism, or do we become defensive and attack with our own criticisms in return?

Let's Talk

How can we improve our patterns of criticizing each other? How can we improve our patterns of accepting criticism from each other?

Let's Do

The next time one of us is being critical, let's take the time to review the situation. Let's look at how the criticism was delivered and how it was received. Let's discuss our feelings, perspectives, and options. Let's try to determine what each of us can do to eliminate the cause for that particular criticism.

Let's Pray

We know we're not perfect, Lord, but we can expect too much from each other at times. We become impatient and critical.

Teach us to be kind and gentle with our criticism. Guide us in offering constructive criticism — always with the good of each other at heart.

Open our hearts to receive criticism with gratitude. Let us be mature enough to accept each other's critical advice without feeling hurt or insulted.

Teach us, Lord, to see and accept criticism as an opportunity for learning and for deepening our love and respect for each other.

Thank you, merciful God, for the gift of wisdom.

ENJOYING YOUR SEXUALITY

There was a time when the subject of sex was rarely discussed. Today, it is openly discussed, studied, surveyed, examined, analyzed, and exploited. Sex and sexuality have been demystified, despiritualized, and liberated so extensively that they often cause problems where no problems should exist.

"When I read the results of some surveys," one young wife declares, "I often wonder what's wrong with my husband and me. We don't even come close to what the surveys insist is the norm."

Statistics can be misinterpreted, deceiving, and wrong. If a husband and wife are satisfied with their sexuality, it doesn't matter how far away — or how near — they are to the so-called norm. Too often a couple will worry about how well they are performing rather than being concerned with the sacred love and pleasure they are sharing.

Many people have trouble accepting occasional performance failures caused by ordinary conditions like sickness, stress, or fatigue. Sometimes couples are simply out of tune with each other, and their moments of sexual sharing are less than satisfying. This, too, is nothing to cause alarm.

Beyond Being Naked

There are times, of course, when couples run into valid problems. An open and honest discussion, with respect and sensitivity, will help them view the problem more realistically. This calls for the couple to go beyond merely being physically naked with each other. Discussing sexual concerns calls for a deeper nakedness: a nakedness of heart and soul. In an environment of unconditional trust, the couple has to voice their concerns, share inhibitions, ask questions, share information, and discuss options. They may find this difficult, but ignoring sexual problems is the beginning of alienation.

Husbands and wives often have different opinions as to what is acceptable and what isn't, what is pleasurable and what isn't, what is appropriate and what isn't, what is comfortable and what isn't. There are few absolute rights and wrongs in lovemaking; there are merely rights and wrongs for each couple to decide upon together. When a couple tries to be sensitive to each other's needs, feelings, and desires, the act of sexual love is a beautiful expression of intimacy and covenantal fidelity.

Key Guidelines

A better title for this section might be "Debunking the Myths of Sex." Our culture has propagated many myths about men, women, and sexuality — myths that do much damage in the light of reality.

Don't automatically assume that you know what each other likes. Don't try to read each other's mind when it comes to your sexual expressions. Don't hesitate to tell each other what you enjoy doing and having done to you. A major myth endorsed by our culture is that men automatically know what women enjoy and all women enjoy the same things. Neither is true. Gender and personality differences play a major role in sexuality.

Be sensitive to each other's intensity of sexual desire. One of the main concerns that eventually develops in a marriage is the change in the intensity of desire. Modern movies portray high levels of desire; arousal is stimulated by the mere sight of a bed. For many, this isn't the case. Granted, one of you may have a higher degree of arousal than the other — and it isn't always the husband. A satisfying compatibility can be achieved if the more sexual partner makes an effort to be caring, patient, understanding, and encouraging rather than demanding and demeaning.

Don't give your lovemaking leftover time. Make sexual intimacy a priority in your relationship. There are many jokes about the lack of interest in sex after marriage. Granted, the passion of your first encounters does dwindle as you adjust to married life. This is not a loss, however. Your love matures with time, as does your sexuality. The passion becomes less a raging fire and more a warm, quiet, perpetual flame. If your lovemaking suffers because of your busy lifestyles, resort to planning — and the planning of romantic encounters is the responsibility of *both* of you.

Some people feel that their sex life should be totally spontaneous. If it is, all well and good. But if it doesn't happen to be, there's nothing wrong with setting a specific time aside for each other — and then making that time meaningful and romantic.

Give and receive love in your sexual expression. There's a danger of becoming selfish in your sexual expressions — especially if you regard intercourse as recreation or an act of sex rather than an act of love. With such an attitude, you may be tempted to use each other for your own gratification. Such self-centeredness reduces physical expressions to a meaningless response to a physical urge. Genuine love-making, on the other hand, is sacred. It involves the whole person, freely and totally, giving and receiving love and pleasure.

Let's Think

Do we regard the act of sexual love as merely a marital right or as a beautiful gift of God?

Are we able to become more than physically naked with each other? Are we able to share our deepest inhibitions, fears, questions, fantasies, and joys regarding sexuality? If not, why?

Do we take our occasional failures too seriously?

Do we forget that hugging, cuddling and being affectionate throughout the day are an important part of love-making?

Let's Talk

What things do we especially enjoy about our love-making? What things make us uncomfortable?

Let's Do

Let's openly discuss any sexual problems we're concerned about.

Let's set aside time for sexually expressing our love to each other. Let's take turns planning how to make it special.

Let's Pray

Bless our acts of love, Lord. Let us always be able to express our sexual love for each other in ways that are gentle, respectful, and pleasurable for both of us.

Don't let us ever misuse the sacred privilege of sexual expression by being demanding or demeaning.

Lord, you are love. Teach us to love with sensitivity, courage, and honesty. Take our inhibitions from us and fill us with intimate delight and delightful intimacy.

Thank you, Lord, for the warmth and comfort we find in each other's arms.

TAKING TIME
FOR PERSONAL PURSUITS

L iz doesn't think her husband is being fair. "Bill goes to a woodworking class on Monday evenings, plays racquetball on Tuesdays and Thursdays, and then goes out to play poker with friends almost every other Friday evening. We spent more evenings together when we were dating than we do now that we're married."

This is an area of sharp tension in a lot of marriages. Some newlyweds have a hard time adjusting their social schedules to their new lifestyle. Some people are actually obsessed with certain activities: jogging, working out, volunteering, hobbies, sports. Their attitudes often put a heavy strain on their primary relationships.

The Balancing Act

Married couples need a certain amount of time for personal pursuits. Couples need to be involved in the broader world — with friends, hobbies, or church and civic activities

— to balance the essence of their intimacy. No single relationship provides an individual with every need. Friends, relatives, coworkers, peers, and personal interests bring symmetry to a relationship. The commitment is not damaged or diminished as a result; it is enriched. Growth and integration cannot happen in a vacuum. The couple needs what friends and interests offer. The key is balance.

Key Guidelines

Some couples struggle for years trying to establish this balance. It calls for good timing and mutual respect for what the personal pursuits entail. Here are a few guidelines that will make your adjustment easier.

Think of each other first. Every decision you make for the rest of your life must be weighed within the context of the covenant you have chosen to share. Your whole way of thinking has to shift from single to couple. Certain activities, for example, that you both enjoyed before you were married are simply no longer appropriate as married persons. Late nights at the singles bars and weekends away with your friends are examples of recreations that do not align with marriage. The two of you are best friends — and this friendship takes precedence. This is a major adjustment for most couples. It will take time, honest dialogue, and tremendous measures of sensitivity.

Review your friendships. Many couples are fortunate to have mutual friends, married and single, with whom they continue to relate. If your friendships are not mutual, take the time to describe what your primary friendships were during your single years. Introduce each other to these special people and work toward integrating your friendships into your marriage.

Respect each other's individuality. There will be people and activities that you simply do not enjoy together. These need not become obstacles to your intimacy. Enjoy your personal friends and activities to a degree that respects your marriage. Then come back together to share your experiences. You'll discover another dimension to the bond you share.

Let's Think

Do we go out too often without each other? Do we stay out too late with our friends?

Do we choose companions and activities that are not appropriate for married persons?

Do we offer each other patient reassurance when friends or activities seem to interfere with our relationship?

Let's Talk

What friends do we have in common? Are they respectful of our marriage? What friends do we have individually? Are they respectful of our marriage?

What activities do we enjoy separately? Do they threaten or enrich our marriage?

Let's Do

Let's list the activities we each like. Then let's discuss the fairness of each activity and decide which ones should be eliminated, which should be included in our individual schedules, and which we can do together.

Let's Pray

Let us realize, Lord, that we need time to pursue our own interests. Teach us to be generous and respectful as we each pursue these interests.

Lord, help us to be fair about the amount of time we take for our own personal activities. We don't want to take unfair advantage of each other.

Give us the wisdom, maturity, and selflessness to work out a fair and compatible schedule with each other.

And, Lord, bless our friendship with warmth and intimacy.

SHARING
HOUSEHOLD CHORES

Terry hates Saturday mornings. "That's when Steve and I do most of our household chores, and that's when we have most of our arguments."

Nobody likes to do chores. Daily living, however, demands they be done. Those sharing life in community have to work out a fair and effective routine.

"I get up early on weekends," says Steve, "and start right in on whatever needs to be done. I want to get everything over with so we can have some relaxing time later in the day. But Terry wants to sleep in. By the time she has breakfast and gets moving, I've finished half the chores."

"The easy half," Terry sharply interjects. "He usually leaves the messiest jobs for me to do."

Developing a System

Dick and Amanda had similar arguments during their first year of marriage. They have developed a system, however, that fairly divides the workload. They each do jobs they specifically don't mind doing and divide the unpleasant chores between them. Although Amanda also enjoys sleeping later on Saturday mornings, she is motivated to get moving by their agreement to treat themselves to lunch at a favorite restaurant when the chores are finished.

There are times when working overtime or ill health makes it necessary for one of them to take on a few extra chores. There are also times when one, feeling unusually energetic, will finish first and offer to help the other. This is partnership!

The Procrastinator

A big argument instigator in marriage is the habit of procrastinating. Evelyn is married to Jim, a procrastinator, and finds herself nagging a great deal of the time. Although Jim can admit that Evelyn's nagging is probably justified, he still responds to it with resentment.

If procrastinators would simply take responsibility for their irresponsibility, the tension may be relieved. Yet, apologies don't get much work done, and neither do anger and nagging.

If one of you is a procrastinator, admit to it. Look around and see the near chaos that procrastination can wreak. Respect the partnership dimension of running a household and renew your attempts to be more responsible.

When trying to motivate a procrastinator, harsh accusations and demands will lead nowhere. Saying "You would make me so happy if you would finish painting the cupboards this weekend" is far more inviting than a harassing statement like "Why in the world do you have to take so long to finish such a small job?"

Key Guidelines

It is unjust and unloving for one of you to carry a heavier burden when it comes to household chores. In trying to work out an acceptable system, keep the following guidelines in mind.

Confront indirectly when a direct confrontation may be nonproductive. When the same chore-related issue continues to cause tension, try writing a note rather than talking about it. Patience and a little humor keep the issue in perspective, and results are far more likely. Avoiding a face-to-face confrontation may mean avoiding an argument.

Find a middle ground when your expectations differ. Discord may arise when there's a big difference between your concepts of neatness. There's bound to be trouble when a very neat person marries a naturally messy one.

Make a sincere attempt to meet each other halfway. If the neater person becomes a little less meticulous and the messy person tries to be a little more tidy-conscious, a more peaceful coexistence can probably be achieved.

Compromise. If spotless rooms and a perfectly manicured lawn — or messy rooms and a ragged lawn — interfere with the enjoyment of your lives, readjust your thinking. Decide just how much neatness is necessary. Most couples can agree that the quality of their relationship should be given preference over the quality of their living room and lawn.

Explore your options. There are many ways to get household chores done that leave both of you off the hook. You might give neighborhood youngsters an opportunity to earn a little spending money by letting them mow, rake, clean the garage, wash the car, scrub floors, scour baths, or paint the porch. Check the classified ads; there are small cottage industries that offer excellent cleaning services at reasonable costs.

Let's Think

Do we have an adequate system for getting chores done? Do we praise each other for a job well done? Do we perform chores with a charitable attitude?

Let's Talk

Is it possible to eliminate some of our household chores — or at least cut back on how frequently they need to be done?

Is there a reward system we can develop that motivates us to get everything done?

Let's Do

Let's draw up a list of chores that have to be done each week and decide which of us should handle which jobs.

Let's Pray

Remind us, Lord, to be fair about helping each other with the routine chores we need to do to run our household.

Grace us with the generosity to do our part — and more when needed.

Don't let us nag each other; don't let us provoke each other to nag. Give us the energy and perseverance to do our part and the courage to insist on equality.

Thank you, all-loving God, for the comfort of our home.

COPING WITH
EVERYDAY PROBLEMS

K eith complains that his wife worries too much. "She'll turn an ordinary situation into a problem just so she has something to worry about. She makes a big deal out of nothing."

Keith's wife is a compulsive worrier. Keith, on the other hand, has a laid-back personality. He often misses a problem when, in fact, a valid one does exist.

We all fall somewhere between these extremes. Because couples react to problems differently, they often have trouble accepting each other's way of perceiving the situation and coping with its complexities.

To Keith's wife, every little conflict or matter of indecision is an overwhelming problem that deserves hours of intense worry. It's hard for him to give his wife the support she needs to get through a difficult situation. To Keith, these situations are merely a part of ordinary life, taken in stride each day. It's unlikely that either will change their orientation.

Mutual Ground

"When Janet is worried about something, she talks about it constantly," her husband, Joe, declares. "I don't quite understand why she has to keep discussing things as much as she does."

Janet, on the other hand, doesn't understand why Joe seldom talks about his problems. "I guess he thinks it's manly to be self-reliant. He prefers to solve his problems alone rather than discuss them with others."

Although Joe gets a bit annoyed with Janet, he usually takes the time to listen to her problems. She, in turn, tries to help him by expressing her availability in the event he needs someone to talk to. She doesn't harass him or nag him to share his concerns. Nor does she offer advice when Joe finally opens up to her. If he asks for her thoughts, Janet respectfully responds with honesty and objectivity.

Most couples enjoy some measure of mutual ground. They find it easy to help each other with main concerns. Although they can't solve each other's problems, they lend support, sympathy (perhaps even empathy), and encouragement. They don't resent being a sounding board for each other when the occasion arises.

Key Guidelines

Besides being a sounding board or clearinghouse for each other's problems, there are other ways you can help each other cope with everyday problems.

Be especially responsible with regard to routine concerns. When it's obvious, for example, that Joe is struggling with an important decision concerning his business, Janet goes out of her way to take care of small family and household problems by herself.

Recognize the gifts in everyday problems. A life without some worry is far from reality. The day-to-day concerns are part of the ingredients that enrich your bond. Daily worries give you common ground for getting in touch with the friendship and covenant you share.

Be comfortable living without a solution to every problem. Not every problem has a solution. Some problems must be accepted and lived with. It is then that the support of a spouse is invaluable.

Let's Think

Are we too negative in dealing with our day-to-day problems? Do we ignore or belittle each other's concerns?

Do we value the power of daily prayer?

Let's Talk

What can we do to support each other when one of us is especially burdened with a concern?

Let's Do

When one of us is dealing with a problem, let's join hands and pray.

Let's be more peaceful with the problems that have no solutions.

Let's Pray

Lord, when worries come up and we get annoyed with each other, teach us compassion and enduring patience. Teach us to be sensitive and kind, to listen attentively to each other when worries press in around us.

Grant us, Lord, the strength, patience, determination, and unswerving faith to cope with all the difficult problems and decisions in our lives. Let us always be consoled by the knowledge that you are constantly with us to comfort us, guide us, and help us.

Thank you, Lord, for the gift of faith we share.

GETTING ALONG
WITH YOUR IN-LAWS

During the first few years of their marriage, Phil and Chris experienced problems with their respective in-laws. They both came from close-knit families that celebrated every birthday and holiday together. In addition to special events, their families often planned family outings and expected all the children to attend.

Phil always left Chris with the unpleasant chore of contacting the families when they couldn't attend a family affair. This was especially frustrating to Chris. She felt that Phil should explain to his family and she would explain to her family. Phil, on the other hand, was aggravated with Chris's habit of planning more get-togethers with her family than with his.

Finally, they addressed the problem. They discussed it with each other and with their parents. They worked out a method that respected the couple's privacy and freedom and the families' desires to have the two of them join their special events. Their discussions made both Chris and Phil more sensitive to the importance of dividing their time equally between families while respecting their need to begin establishing their own traditions.

Change the Way You Listen

Dan and Pat had a different problem with their respective in-laws. Their parents were ready, willing, and eager to give guidance and advice — sometimes critical advice — to their newly married offspring. The young couple had many bitter arguments about this, until the two of them finally took the time to discuss their dilemma.

Pat's easygoing approach to life came in handy. She explained to Dan that their parents meant well and that their advice was an attempt to be helpful. She reasoned that it was probably difficult for parents who were accustomed to giving daily advice to their children in their growing years to completely refrain from doing so after they were married.

Viewing their parents' suggestions as well-meant advice rather than criticism equipped Pat and Dan to better cope with the situation. They opened their attitude to their parents' advice and listened with a different orientation. Instead of reacting with resentment, as they did in the past, Dan and Pat tried to respond with kindness, tact, and appreciation. They remained noncommittal in their responses, however: "We'll be sure to consider your suggestions when it comes to our decision on this" or "Thank you for your advice, but we aren't sure that's the best way for us to handle our decision."

Of course, there are people who are much too outspoken and far too critical. There are some who have faults that are extremely annoying. In such cases, refrain from criticizing each other's family. No one is perfect — including yourselves. Is it possible to accept and live with the faults and imperfections of your in-laws for the sake of harmony in your marriage? Appreciate each other's struggle to be patient and tolerant. See an opportunity in the situation to love each other heroically and unconditionally.

When dealing with annoying in-laws, remember that they are the people responsible for giving you each other. Something they did has contributed to the people you are, the precious and appealing mate you are for each other. One can always appreciate in-laws for that.

Respect the Intimate Friendship You Share

Before she married Jim, Jill had a close relationship with her mother. Together, they discussed their problems, down to the finest and most intimate detail. Jill continued this intimacy with her mother after her marriage. She gave her mother a detailed update of everything she and Jim did and said.

Jill was not respecting the friendship she shared with her beloved. She left herself open to biased advice and disregarded the integrity of her intimacy with Jim. She risked giving her mother a negative image of Jim, an image that could lead to hostility and distrust.

Keep your differences within the walls of your home. Discuss and resolve your differences between the two of you, not with friends, family, and in-laws. If one or both of you had confidantes before you were married, discuss how the nature of those relationships impacts — or could impact — your marriage. Respect your marriage; explain to your friends and relatives that the most intimate friendship in your life is now the one you share with your spouse. There are some things that should be kept strictly within the sacred bounds of that friendship. Genuine friends and relatives, ones that support your marriage and foster the bond, will deeply respect you for this kind of honesty.

"I would really love to talk to Tom about all my concerns and interests," says Susan. "After all, he really is my best friend. But he doesn't seem to want to take the time. So I usually talk to my sister about them — and I end up discussing a lot of private stuff. I know Tom would be upset if he knew some of the things I tell her."

Keeping certain things to yourselves requires patience and availability. Don't lose sight of each other's need for deep soul-baring talk. Saying "Let's talk more about this" is another way of saying "I love you."

Let's Think

Do we criticize each other's family, or do we look upon our in-laws' failings as a challenge we can respond to out of love for each other?

Are we considerate and respectful of each other's feelings and the need to talk about those feelings? Do we make ourselves available for such talking?

Do we remain faithful to each other by respecting the intimacy of our friendship?

Let's Talk

What amount of time is a "fair amount" to spend with each of our families? Do we need to make some changes in how and when we spend time with our families?

What subjects deserve the respect of being kept between us?

Let's Do

Let's work out a tentative and fair schedule for spending time with each other's family. Let's occasionally invite each other's family to our home.

Let's explain to our families and friends the primacy of our friendship.

Let's Pray

Help us, Lord, to treat each other with respect, consideration, and graciousness. Fill our hearts with love for the persons who gave life to us.

Let us overlook our in-laws' faults; let us be generous. Teach us to love them as Christ loves them: just as they are. Don't let us ever get into the habit of criticizing them — or of responding to them with anger.

Open our hearts to see our in-laws' advice as loving concern rather than criticism.

Thank you, Creator of Life, for participating with them in giving us life.

ESTABLISHING YOUR BUDGET

When a husband and wife have different attitudes on how to handle their finances, problems arise. What one may think is thrifty, the other may perceive as miserly. What one may consider reasonable, the other may find extravagant.

Some couples run into problems because they have a "mine-and-yours" attitude regarding money. What she brings into the budget is hers, and she can do what she wants with it; what he brings in is his, and he can do what he wants with his. Such an attitude is detrimental to a union as intimate as marriage.

Other couples operate on a "more/less" basis of handling money: the one who earns the most exercises the most control over decisions pertaining to money. Other couples decide that one of them will completely control the money and take care of the budget, regardless of who earns the most.

None of these models is reliable. When two people marry, they become financial partners who work together to achieve mutual goals within a sound budget. Who earns the most, who needs the most, or who has the better financial wherewithal are not adequate reasons to turn the budget over to one person. Money is a sacred resource that calls for the couple's careful and prayerful management.

George is an engineer; Judy is a hostess in a restaurant. "Since George earns a lot more money than I do, he feels that he should make all the decisions about how we spend our money." George leaves Judy with little to say about their finances. She is completely unaware of their overall financial picture.

When one of you is completely responsible for the management of financial resources, your relationship enters a "high-risk" zone. The environment is ripe for arguments, resentments, distrust, and misjudgment. In our culture, money means power — and eventually, financial control in the hands of one person will begin to erode at the mutuality of your marriage.

Key Guidelines

Keep the following guidelines in mind as you discuss your financial resources.

Agree on financial limits and goals. Before they're married, couples often fail to define their lifestyle and financial needs, wants, and ambitions. "I never realized that our desires and goals are so different," declares Maria. "Whenever we have a little extra money, Peter wants to blow it on expensive theater tickets or sports events. I'd rather buy some household appliance that we need or just save it for a special trip or some crisis that may come up." Peter also feels that it's necessary to get a new car with air conditioning every couple of years, while Maria thinks a stripped-down used model is good enough.

If you haven't done it yet, do it now. Seriously discuss your financial priorities. Agree on limits and goals. When you decide and compromise on these issues, you can more effectively work out a successful budget.

Budget together. Your budget must include regular monthly expenses (rent or mortgage payments, loan payments, utility bills, food, automobile expenses, insurance, and so forth). Next, determine an amount for household furnishings, auto and commuting expenses, clothing, medical expenses, gifts, and recreation.

You should always allow for some savings — no matter how small — for emergencies and major expenses you can anticipate in the years ahead: buying a home, having a child, extending your education.

Make adjustments as they are needed. You will make mistakes when you plan your first budget. Be flexible. Change the budget when you find it isn't working. At times, job changes and unforeseen expenses will also mean that the budget has to be reworked. Be alert and prioritize your time to periodically review your financial resources and how you are respecting those resources.

Develop a system. How will your salary(ies) be handled? Should the earnings go into joint or separate accounts? What should these accounts be used for?

Most couples divide their payroll check(s) into several categories: a checking account for immediate and monthly expenses, a savings account for occasional major expenses or unforeseen financial needs, and cash on hand for day-today operating expenses. You should each keep a certain amount of cash for yourself for simple wants and needs as they come up.

"I have to ask Lois for every dollar I spend," complains Jerry. "It isn't that she doesn't give me what I need, it's just that it's terribly demeaning to have to ask for money every time I need it." No spouse should be forced to ask for every single dollar that's spent on personal needs.

Know your financial picture at all times. Although one of you may actually pay the bills and keep financial and tax records, both of you should have a clear understanding of your financial position at all times. You should know exactly how and if your budget is working and where you stand financially. Go over your bills together each month.

Agree on the use of credit cards. Problems will arise when one of you wants to use the credit card only for large purchases and the other insists on using it for everything. Remember that high finance charges can nullify any bargain items you decide to "card."

The use of credit cards may tempt you to live beyond your means. It's much wiser to use your charge cards for convenience purposes only, eliminating the need to carry large sums of money around. Pay off your entire balance each month.

Shop together. One of you may hate shopping. For your own education, however, spend an entire month doing routine shopping together. Develop an appreciation for the cost of food, toiletries, household-cleaning products, laundry items, and dry-cleaning expenses. Without this appreciation, there remains the danger of arguing about the extravagance — or imagined extravagance — of each other's spending habits.

Budget for entertainment and charity. Even when your budget is tight, allot a percentage for entertainment and charitable purposes. Your financial resources are gifts from the Author of Life, who intends for you to enjoy life. Respect your gifts; share them generously. Give to your relationship by budgeting for entertainment and give to others by lightening their financial burdens.

Money Is Only Part of the Picture

Your contribution of personal earnings to the overall stability of your relationship is not the entire picture. Both of you invest valuable time, skills, and energy in maintaining the life you share; your financial resources is only one dimension of what you each bring to your marriage. Since you committed all you are and all you have to the relationship, you are entitled to participate equally in every phase of daily living — including financial management. A nonworking spouse provides as much support to the overall good of the marriage as does the spouse who is in the work force bringing home a paycheck. You both are entitled to an equal voice in decisions regarding financial matters.

Let's Think

Do we share and discuss budget concerns and financial decisions on a regular basis?

Do we respect each other's contributions to the overall, day-to-day management of the life we share?

Do we argue over finances because one or both of us fails to respect our financial resources?

Let's Talk

How can we best budget our financial resources? What can we eliminate from our budget or reduce as an expenditure? What percentage of our financial resources do we use for entertainment and charitable causes?

Let's Do

Let's go over our budget at least once a month. Let's make it an enjoyable evening by combining it with a carry-out dinner that we can eat picnic-style on a blanket on the living-room floor.

Let's go to the library and pick up some books on budgeting or attend a class on budgeting and household financing.

Let's Pray

Thank you, Lord, for the financial gifts you have generously provided. Help us make wise and mature decisions concerning the management of our money. When we argue about finances, draw our hearts together as one.

Let us be fair and open with each other. Let us respect each other's needs. Keep us free from the desire to exercise power by wielding financial control.

Grant us, Lord, the gifts of good judgment and generosity.

GROWING
IN YOUR MARRIAGE

L aura was dissatisfied with life. When she met John and fell in love, she finally began to experience a sense of contentment. John was the man of her dreams: romantic, kind, attentive, and deeply in love with her. She was sure that John would always meet her needs and make her happy.

Shortly after they were married, however, Laura's discontentment returned. The romantic attentiveness of courtship gave way to the demands of John's profession and the ordinary business of daily living. Once again, Laura was faced with her own inner lack of peace.

Laura had expected John to hand her happiness on a silver platter. She expected marriage to be a world of perpetual romance and satisfaction.

Your Happiness Is Your Happiness

No one can give another person a sense of contentment and happiness. That responsibility rests within each individual. It's unfair to expect a spouse to compensate for his or her partner's negative attitudes and discontentment. Such an expectation is not centered in a genuine caring for the beloved; it is a love that centers on self. No one can magically make another's life happy. Yet, many tend to cling to this attitude; it's easier to blame another when life falls flat.

When each partner in a marriage accepts responsibility for his or her own faults, deficiencies, and limitations, the marriage begins to thrive. Two people who love themselves and each other and hold optimistic orientations toward life can enjoy a fulfilling intimate relationship.

Successful marriages are characterized by the growth of each individual. "What I like most about my marriage," declares Janice, "is that we give each other space. We're interested in each other's well-being, and we share a lot of life. But we don't feel limited by that. Rather, we feel free to grow and change and learn, knowing that we're loved." Though they have many interests in common, Janice and her husband have many individual interests as well. They allow each other time for personal pursuits and make it a point to encourage and support each other.

"He appreciates the satisfaction I get out of painting," continues Janice. "As a result, he often goes out of his way to make it possible for me to attend classes. And although he's not as crazy about art as I am, he tries to share my interest by occasionally accompanying me to an art show."

This couple recognizes the importance of nurturing both their individuality and their oneness. They appreciate the changes that occur as a relationship matures. "What makes our marriage so good," remarks Janice, "is that I am always finding something new to love in Doug. I don't think we should ever stop searching for something new to love in each other."

Healthy Interdependence

A balanced sense of dependence and independence is another necessary ingredient in a mature and growing relationship.

Robert has always been an extremely independent individual. He pursues his interests and activities with a fervor that leaves his wife, Carol, feeling isolated. Robert makes plans and decisions that should be made with Carol's input. Carol resents Robert's extreme sense of independence, and their marriage is deprived of the opportunity to mature.

Eileen, on the other hand, is overly dependent. Although she is a skillful driver, she prefers that Greg chauffeur her. She depends on Greg to handle their finances, manage their household, and make arrangements for their social outings. Greg often feels burdened and constricted by Eileen's dependence.

Too much dependence or independence in an intimate relationship can inhibit the growth of the partners and the relationship itself. If a marriage is to succeed, a healthy interdependence is essential. The couple sharing daily responsibilities, concerns, and pleasures while developing individual responsibility can count on a balance of dependence and independence.

Let's Think

Do we enjoy a healthy interdependence? Do we take responsibility for our own contentment in life? Are there times when we rely on each other too much — or not enough?

Let's Talk

How can we improve our support of each other?
How can we foster interdependence in our marriage?

Let's Do

Let's celebrate each other's accomplishments by doing something special when one of us excels in something.

Let's Pray

Hold our hearts in peace, Lord. Don't let us blame each other for our own shortcomings and dissatisfactions. Help us face life with a sense of responsibility for our own happiness, a mature and positive attitude, and a well-developed sense of humor.

Show us how to bring about interdependence in our marriage. Bless us with wisdom and love to respect each other's individuality and value our oneness.

Thank you, Lord, for the strengths and weaknesses that make us a good team.

BUILDING A
SPIRITUAL RELATIONSHIP

Many Christian couples separate the spiritual part of their life from the other aspects of living. They place spirituality into a separate little compartment and dip into it when problems become overwhelming. When all else fails, some couples turn to a means of help and support beyond themselves.

As spiritual beings, however, we long for an integrated life. We want life to hold promise, purpose, and meaning.

Your Third Partner

There is a third "participant" in every Christian marriage. This Partner deeply loves the couple and cares for their welfare. This Partner is always available to comfort, strengthen, support, and guide them with hope and wisdom. Developing a closer relationship with this Partner enriches the sacred bond the couple shares. This Partner, of course, is God.

Your Faith Community

Join a faith community or continue to participate in the one you're affiliated with. Actively participate in the life of your church community. Attend services, participate in the education and charitable programs the church supports, and contribute to the church's financial needs.

Regularly celebrating with your faith community is important. Although services may at times seem boring or irrelevant, they contribute to the ongoing spiritual maturity of your marriage. In the embrace of the community, where your bond is recognized and respected, your covenant takes on genuine meaning. It becomes more than a shared life; it becomes a partnership with the Author of Life. You realize grace from the presence of God in the community and contribute to that mystery for the good of others. Your marriage needs the support of the community — and the community needs you. Your marriage is a powerful witness to the unconditional love of God.

Joining your brothers and sisters in Christ at the table of the Lord nourishes your souls. By participating in the social and spiritual events of your church, you experience the familial alliance you share with others in the Body of Christ.

Prayer

Most of us pray, but we pray sporadically. We tend to treat God as a power enthroned in heaven, waiting to be called upon when our burdens get to be too much for us to handle. We often fail to see God as our perpetual shepherd, guide, light, confidante, and intimate partner. Understanding some of the basics of prayer will help you integrate spirituality in the overall fabric of your lives.

God initiates; you respond. God is not an intruder. Although God initiates a longing for communion in the depths of your souls, it is, nonetheless, your responsibility to respond, "Yes, come, Lord." If you choose to ignore God, you lock yourself away from the source of peace that can sustain you through the complex challenges of marriage.

God participates in your daily life. A simple one-line prayer brings God to the forefront of your mind and heart: "What a beautiful sunset, Lord. I thank you for the chance to share this with my spouse." "I'm having trouble doing my job today — please help me with it." "That music is great, Lord. Enjoy it with me." "That music is driving me crazy, Lord. Bless me with tolerance."

Pray together. By talking to God about mutual feelings and concerns, you are drawn into a deeper and more intimate relationship with your third Partner and with each other. This may be difficult for you at first. Perhaps you have inhibitions about prayer in general. Maybe you think you'll appear too holy holy. Perhaps you're uncomfortable praying together. Many couples claim that there simply isn't enough time to pray together.

A little planning, a little initiative, and perhaps a bit of coaxing will help the two of you overcome these common struggles with shared prayer. Your lack of know-how can actually be a great asset; it can be channeled into a freeing form of self-expression. The lack of time can be eliminated by setting aside a few minutes a day to join hands and simply become aware of God's wondrous participation in the love you share. Prayer does not have to be long and structured to be enriching.

Sally was determined to start a daily practice of praying

with her husband. When he balked at her suggestion to pray together, she began saying a short prayer after getting into bed each night. After a few days, her husband began responding with a simple and respectful "Amen" when it was evident that she had closed her prayer. Eventually, Sally's husband began to add a few of his own comments to God.

Prayer intensifies your intimacy. Praying out loud together is the most direct way of blessing a misunderstanding and celebrating reconciliation. "Lord, we've argued. We've hurt each other deeply. Teach us to soothe each other's hurts. Give us the love and understanding we need to avoid hurting each other in the future."

Through your prayers, you can share a problem or get help in making a decision. You can apologize, forgive, and show your love and concern for each other in ways no other means accomplishes. The awesome grace of God is acknowledged in your midst, loving each of you as you love each other.

A prayer such as "Thank you, Lord, for helping Mary put up with my crabbiness today" shows a wife that her husband acknowledges his faults. She is touched by his honesty and quickly opens her heart in understanding and forgiveness.

When you are in the midst of a misunderstanding, "Help us, Lord, accept and understand each other's point of view" shows your willingness to work through the issue with respect.

Imagine your spouse holding you in the quiet softness of approaching sleep and hearing, "Lord, thank you for blessing us with a life together. I treasure the love we share more than anything else." What a gentle way to place your love in the lap of God.

The essence of your prayer can come from many sources.
The common events of your day, a shared desire or dream, or a mutual or personal problem are excellent prayer ingredients. Using Scripture spiritual reading or a book of prayer for married couples will also help enrich your prayer. *Prayers for Married Couples* (Liguori Publications), for example, helps make it easier for a couple to pray aloud together and can promote a more open and expressive sharing of attitudes and feelings.

Couples who persevere in the practice of praying out loud together eventually find their prayers becoming not only conversations with God but also a means of communicating with each other.

"My husband and I have been praying together for almost a year," one young wife explains. "We've become much more understanding of each other. When we pray, a lot of our hurts and fears and doubts come out. As a result, it's easier for us to discuss things we were uncomfortable about. We talk a lot more about our goals and dreams, something we didn't do before."

Prayer will draw you closer together in a more intimate and understanding relationship. Prayer will enrich your lives by developing and deepening your union with our Creator.

Let's Think

Do we appreciate the power of prayer in our marriage? Do we thank God for all our blessings?

Do we share our spiritual beliefs, our yearnings, our doubts, our faith, our dreams?

Let's Talk

How can we establish the habit of praying together?

Why do we go to church? Do we understand how the faith community supports us and how we support it?

Let's Do

Let's say one-line prayers throughout the day. Let's occasionally say them out loud in each other's presence.

Let's say a small prayer in the morning as we begin the day and before dinner each evening.

Let's attend a Marriage Encounter weekend or make a retreat for married couples.

Let's read a small passage from Scripture each day.

Let's Pray

As we join our hands and voices in prayer, Lord, let us draw closer to each other and to you. Keep our hearts open to your constancy and goodness.

We acknowledge our dependence on you. We are confident in your fidelity to us. We trust in your care, wisdom, and strength.

Enter our marriage, Lord, and dwell at the very center of it. We place our covenant in your hands.

We praise you, Lord, for you are wondrous, indeed.

More for Married Couples
From Liguori Publications...

Prayers for Married Couples
by Renee Bartkowski

A collection of over 75 brief prayers that express the hopes, the concerns, and the dreams of today's married couples. It helps couples build a more spiritual union—with each other—and with God. **$5.95**

Handbook for Today's Catholic Family
A Redemptorist Pastoral Publication

This popular title is a practical manual for Catholic living that helps families write their own "faith histories" for future generations. Blending the riches of the Gospel with lived Catholic experience, it should be part of every Catholic family library. **$4.95**
Also available in Spanish...**Manual Para La Familia Católica Hispaña de Hoy. $3.95**

Family Planning
A Guide for Exploring the Issues
by Charles and Elizabeth Balsam

Concise and easy to read, this book offers information on family planning methods and discusses related aspects of family life including responsible parenthood, conscience formation, and decision-making. Includes a synopsis of Church teaching, a section "For Men Only," couple-dialogue worksheets, and more. **$1.95**

Order from your local bookstore or write to
Liguori Publications
Box 060, Liguori, MO 63057-9999
*Please add 15% to your total for shipping and handling
($3.50 minimum, $15 maximum).*